The snowball

Written by Wes Magee

Illustrated by Val Biro

Nesta and Ned were little dragons.
One day they flew off
to see Grandma Dragon.

There was snow on Creepy Castle.

There was snow in Wild Wood.

There was snow on the hill.

Nesta and Ned looked down.
They could see Grandma in her cave
and they could see Big Bad Dragon.
'Why is Big Bad Dragon down there?'
said Nesta.

Big Bad Dragon made a big snowball.
He put the snowball in the cave.
'Ha, ha, ha!' said Big Bad Dragon.
'Now Grandma can't get out.'

'Oh no!' said Nesta.

'We have to help Grandma.

Come on, Ned.'

Nesta and Ned flew down to the cave.

'Help! Help!' said Grandma.

Nesta and Ned called to Grandma.

'We will help you.

We will get you out.'

Nesta blew fire on the snowball.
She blew and blew and blew.

Ned blew fire on the snowball.
He blew and blew and blew.

'Now I can get out,' said Grandma.
She was very happy.
But Nesta and Ned were cross.
'We will make a snowball
for that dragon,' said Nesta.

Nesta and Ned made a big snowball.
It went over and over the snow
and down and down the hill.
'Help!' said Big Bad Dragon.

Big Bad Dragon fell down and
the big snowball went over him.

Big Bad Dragon and the snowball
went down and down the hill.

'Ha, ha, ha!' said Nesta and Ned.
'Now it is a very big snowball.'
And they flew off to play
in the snow.